Mostly Bob

Mostly Bob

Tom Corwin

New World Library · Novato, California

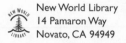
New World Library
14 Pamaron Way
Novato, CA 94949

Library of Congress Cataloging-in-Publication Data

    Corwin, Tom.
    Mostly Bob / Tom Corwin.
        p. cm.
ISBN-13: 978-1-57731-525-4 (hardcover : alk. paper)
1. Dogs–California–Anecdotes. 2. Corwin, Tom. 3. Dog
owners–California–Anecdotes. 4. Human-animal
relationships–California–Anecdotes. I. Title.
SF426.2.C68 2006
636.752'7–dc22

                                        2005022626

First printing, February 2006
ISBN-10 1-57731-525-1
ISBN-13 978-1-57731-525-4

Printed in Canada
♻ 100 percent postconsumer waste recycled paper
🅖 A proud member of the Green Press Initiative
Distributed to the trade by Publishers Group West

10 9 8 7 6 5 4 3 2 1

PROLOGUE

Earlier this year when Bob, my best friend (and golden retriever), died suddenly, I was compelled to write a letter to his friends and family as a toast to his life. He and I were essentially inseparable, and consequently a great number of people had come to know and love him, yet only a few knew his history.

Bob's life was a real tribute to courage, perseverance and the possibility of change. I felt it was only right to share his story and the news of his sad departure with those who had been touched by him. I was devastated by his leaving, and the therapy of paying tribute to his life was good for me as well.

In the following months the letter assumed a life of its own. Many who received it continued to forward it, and I began to receive email from strangers telling me how they too had been touched by the story.

Then, a dear friend, author Leslie McGuirk, insisted that the letter should really be a book. With an immediate sense of how it would look, I became consumed in the creative process of bringing it to life. This is the letter as it was originally written.

Tom Corwin

To all of you who have known and loved Bob,

I am terribly sad to say that
Bob left us Saturday morning.

He was a great source of love, comfort and laughs
to many of us.

He should serve as a powerful reminder to us all
that wounded hearts can, and do, heal.

It seemed to me his story deserved writing down.

He was amazingly successful in changing his own life.

There are not a lot of dogs who can make that claim.

He was a true hero.

As you may know, Bob came to me after nine years
of suffering and neglect.

He had the misfortune of having a dog owner
who had very little understanding
of how to love animals.

He was locked out of the house, and it seemed the only time Bob got attention was when his owner's temper was raging.

As a consequence Bob grew up seeing life through
the narrow eyes of fear and survival.

I knew him for all those years
as the psycho-dog next door.

He was unbathed, smelled bad and looked like hell.

He never set foot on my property.

As much of a dog lover as I am, there was little to love or appreciate about Bob.

If anyone (including myself) tried to walk
onto the neighbor's property and pet him,
he would peer through distrustful eyes, show his teeth,
growl and bark like a rabid animal.

Occasionally when Bob would spend literally hours on end barking next door, I would walk over, brave his threats and try to calm him down.

Sometimes it worked.

I must admit in spite of this
even I couldn't find much to like about Bob.

Then about four and a half years ago,
through sheer genius and determination on Bob's part,
he changed his own life.

He apparently noticed that Bubba, my fifteen-year-old golden retriever, had recently and sadly departed.

(He may also have noticed that for the last year
and a half of Bubba's life I had been carrying him
up my one hundred stairs every day.)

About a month later I looked out the window
and saw Bob on my property.

I remember thinking to myself,
"That's weird, he never steps over the property line."

The next thing I noticed
was when he walked onto my deck
about a week later and lay down.

"Now that's really, really weird."

Then he simply stayed.

I did absolutely nothing to encourage him except offer the simple courtesy of an occasional conversation

— no food, no water, no entry into the house,
he was stinky and strange after all.

But Bob essentially refused to leave.

(Bob had lived his entire life as an outside dog. He slept on an old couch under a covered deck next door. That was about it, plus one bowl of food a day.)

For almost a year and a half
Bob stayed under these conditions.

He would go next door at 6:00 pm for the bowl of food left out for him and be back at 6:05.

This became a practiced routine.

Meanwhile he started following me wherever I went.

For those of you who don't know my house, it has many doors, and Bob began lying outside the one nearest to where I was at all times.

When I was in my office,
he would lie outside the office door.

When I'd go to the kitchen to get a cup of coffee,

he'd run around the house
to the kitchen door
and lie down.

When two minutes later I'd go back into the office,

he'd run around the house and plop down again
outside the French doors to the office.

Off to the studio, there he is again.

He was clearly committed to this plan
and worked it every single day.

He stuck as close to me as he could,
and all I ever offered him was casual interaction.

As time passed, Bob eventually softened.

His narrow eyes and furrowed brow began to relax.

He started to cower less
when a caress of his head was offered.

And after a while he even began to enjoy them.

As this transformation progressed
I felt myself start to care more and more.

After a year and a half
Bob had completed his two-year plan ahead of schedule.

I finally broke down and said,
"Okay, if you insist on being here, you're getting a bath."

I was tired of having a stinky dog around

and with some encouragement from a friend
got over the weirdness of washing the neighbor's dog.

That was the turning point.

Once he was clean and sweet smelling
I felt compelled to cuddle him.

Then I invited him into the house.

I slowly fell in love.

The love grew until there was no containing it,

and in my complete love I wanted Bob to come
with me when I left the house.

(I have always been the kind of dog owner
who takes my dogs everywhere I go.)

When I found myself sneaking Bob to my car,
occasionally hiding behind a tree
to avoid being spotted by his "owner,"

I knew something was very wrong.

After summoning great courage I called Mark

Mark: neighbor, dog "owner"

and said, "I'd like to come over and talk about something."

I walked over with my heart in my throat
and an ache in my stomach.

We sat down and I dove in:

"Mark, I want to talk to you about Red."

(Bob's previous name)

"I think it's time I took over the food and vet bills...."

to which he replied,

"Oh Tom, I figured that a year ago.
He's obviously chosen you."

My heart relaxed
and I felt a deep breath pass through my lips.

Bob and I were official.

I was thrilled and so was Bob.

From that point on
Bob became more loving by the day.

And I felt the blessing of having his beautiful spirit
as my constant companion.

As he started his official travel schedule,
ever by my side, Bob discovered the world.

He went on hikes, to beaches, over bridges,
to fancy restaurants,

to recording sessions and at least twice
got his own personalized laminate at rock concerts
reading, "Bob, V.I.D. — ALL ACCESS."

He evolved into a puddle of love
and shared his immense heart and spirit
every step of the way.

He melted my heart to the core

and took many other prisoners along the way
(you may have been one).

The unconditional love one can have for an animal
is so very close to the best concepts of "God."

I feel so lucky to have known him this way

and to have had the gift of his deep friendship
for the past three years.

It has been joyful.

I hope I can carry some of this
unconditional love forward into the world

with Bob in my heart, rather than by my side.

Right now though,

I am deeply missing the sound of his breath at my feet.

The sad part of the story:

Unfortunately Bob twisted into a spasm of pain
Friday evening

while lying at my feet under the recording console in my studio.

I jumped to the floor and held him.

He relaxed after a few minutes but couldn't get up.

The highly abbreviated version of this story is that we ended up at the pet emergency room at 9:45 pm

and after an exam, blood samples,
X-rays and three hours,

they found that Bob's spleen had "grown to the size of a cantaloupe" and was bleeding.

He was in pain, and the vet said
there was really only one thing to do.

It was now one in the morning.

I lay on the floor with Bob and
cuddled him for over an hour

and then I held him as he left his beautiful body.

What mattered most
was for him to feel the depth of my love
until the last second of his life.

I know he did

— I still feel his.

Lots of love,
Tom and Bob

About the Author

Tom Corwin is a musician and music producer
living in Northern California.